THE HOLY FLIERS

by

Josh Rubin

Known to his grandchildren as

"Pops"

Illustrated by Shira Peled

Mazo Publishers

The Holy Fliers

ISBN: 978-1-956381-36-8

Josh (Yehoshua) Rubin – Copyright © 2023

Also available in Hebrew

Author

Josh (Yehoshua) Rubin
is a Life Coach and Therapist with
a Masters in Counseling.
He is available for coaching
and counseling sessions.

Contact Josh Rubin
WhatsApp: +972504259191
Israel number: 0504259191
Email: yehoshuarubin@gmail.com

Illustrator
Shira Peled: 0559183141

Mazo Publishers
Chaim Mazo, Publisher
www.mazopublishers.com
chaim@mazopublishers.com

Hi – My name is Shira, that's me on the red mattress. This is a story about my grandfather. We call him "Pops."

Are you ready to hear the story?

Well – when I was growing up,
school was busy and home was also busy.
But home was fun busy. I spent a lot of time playing tag
with my sister and brothers and sliding down the stairs on a mattress.
Busy, busy, busy... But sunsets were different. They weren't busy.
Sunsets were a peaceful time.

Sometimes, after supper, Avi, Shayna, Yonatan and I would bring our blankets out to the back porch, lie down and watch the sunset with Aba and Ima.

(That's me with the star blanket. As you can see, Yonatan stole my pillow. After a few years, I forgave him.)

It was a time of being close and together. It was a time of snuggling in a blanket when the wind was strong.

It was a peaceful time. I mean it was peaceful once we had arranged our blankets, stopped fighting about pillows and who was kicking whom. After all that, we finally settled down to quietly watch the sun sink, and the moon rise.

It was also story time. Our parents would take turns telling us stories. This story is about one of those times.

Aba was deciding which story to tell us. While we waited, we pulled the covers up close because it was so windy.

It was so windy that we could see how the strong winds pushed the clouds and hid the moon.

Shayna, my older sister, teased me and said, "That's it, no more moon."

"No more moon?" Aba asked. "This reminds me of a story and it is a story about Pops."

Pops is our grandfather.

We like hearing stories about Pops because he did so many interesting things. He traveled to many places, made things out of wood, built campfires for us, wrote children's books and loved to dance with Bubzy, our grandmother.

"What connection could there be between Pops and the moon?" I wondered.

Abba continued, "We know Pops today as a successful businessman. Yet once, Pops was young and went to school just like you. School wasn't easy for Pops. He tried to get high grades, but he never did.

Then, in junior high school, things changed.

One day in English class, his teacher, Mrs. Garb said, "Today we will do some creative writing."

Well, you know how creative Pops is, so this cheered him up.

"Today," she continued, "you are going to write about encouragement."

After so many years of getting C's and D's, Pops had a lot to say about how students should be encouraged!

He started to write.

Three pages later he handed in his essay.

But Pops was worried that Mrs. Garb wouldn't like what he wrote. He wrote that sometimes his teachers said some things that were not so nice. Things that made him feel stupid.

Mrs. Garb took his paper, smiled and put it in her bag.

At the next English class, Mrs. Garb handed back everyone's papers and when she gave Pops his paper, he couldn't believe it.

There was a big, red "A" on his paper, and at the bottom of the page Mrs. Garb had written, "Very Good!" in bright red ink.

It was Pops' first "A!" And he really liked seeing "Very Good!" on his paper. He felt warm inside. He said to himself, "This is what encouragement must feel like!"

So, the next day he did something he had never done before. He took a chance and wrote down his thoughts, and then shared them with Mrs. Garb.

Mrs. Garb returned his paper, and once again she had written "Very Good."

Again, he felt warm inside. Again, he felt encouraged.

So, he took another chance and again wrote down his thoughts and handed them in to his teacher. In fact, he did this quite a few times.

Each time Mrs. Garb returned his paper, she had written "Very Good!"

And each "Very Good" felt warm and sweet, like he was eating a fresh chocolate cookie!

After a while, Mrs. Garb asked Pops if he would like to submit one of his poems to a writing contest. As much as he wanted to, Pops was afraid that the judges would not like what he wrote.

Seeing Pops' hesitation, Mrs. Garb said, "I know there's a chance of being disappointed, but your writing is very good. Let's pick one of the poems that is very, very good."

Well, that is exactly what happened. They sent in a poem and guess what ... ***Pops won second place!***

The awards ceremony for the contest winners was held in an auditorium, with extra chairs set up, close to the stage.

The judge's voice was loud and clear, and he read into the microphone what each winner wrote. The judge's careful reading of Pops' poem filled the auditorium and touched his heart.

At that moment, a new thought came to Pops.

After so many years of thinking "I can't," his new thought was "I CAN!"

With "I CAN!" in his mind, Pops got up to receive his prize and handshake. He posed for the winner's picture and soaked up the applause.

Aba asked us, "What do you think Pops felt when he saw that people liked his writing?"

"Warm inside," Avi said.

"Yes," Aba agreed. "Remember how warm we feel when we sit around a campfire on a cool night? Or how tingly the sun feels when it warms us up after a dip in the ocean?"

"That's how Pops felt – All warm and tingly."

Aba paused for a moment, and with a serious look on his face, we could tell that he was thinking about something very important.

"I remember Pops repeating those new words throughout my childhood, whenever I felt down. 'I can, I can, I can!'"

Then Aba looked at all of us and said, "Memorize those two words of encouragement, they'll never disappoint you."

This story could end here, but actually our story is just beginning! Now we are about to learn about Pops and the moon!

After the ceremony, Pops boarded a bus that would take him home. It happened to be that the auditorium was in a very religious neighborhood and there were a lot of Hasidim on the bus. One young Hasid, just a little older than Pops, sat in the seat next to him.

Pops was following the moon through the bus window when he realized the Hasid was talking to him. Seeing Pops' kipa, he asked Pops if he studied Gemara in school, like they did in Yeshiva.

Pops shook his head and said, "No."

The Hasid was quiet for a moment and then said, "Well, if we can't talk about Gemara, let me tell you a story.

Curious, Pops said, "Ok."

Pausing with the story, Aba told us, "Now we are getting really close to the connection between Pops and us sitting here watching the wind pushing the clouds and covering the moon's light.

"You know everyone has their favorite story, one that touches their heart. The story that warms them up. The one that gives them hope when it's dark outside.

"That is exactly what happened when Pops heard the Hasid's story. And it became his favorite heart-warming story. Because it gave him so much hope.

"Days of hope? No.

"Months of hope? No.

"It gave Pops years of hope. Years and years of hope.

"So much hope that Pops has never stopped telling the Hasid's story. It has been 50 years since then. Yet Pops tells it like he heard it yesterday."

"Ok, ok," I interrupted my father's story-telling, "We get how great the story is. So, please tell us the story already."

"I will," Aba said. "First you need to know that Pops gave the story a name. He called it 'The Holy Fliers' and here is the story Pops heard from the Hasid."

The Holy Fliers

There's a special prayer that we say when we first spy the new moon. We want to thank God for, once again, lighting up the dark sky.

One night, a group of Hasidim went outside to say this prayer, *Kiddush Levana* – the Blessing of the Moon.

But they could not find the moon! Thick clouds were covering the moon just like the clouds are right now. And you can't say the blessing until you see the moon.

"Ok," they said to each other, "we will wait until tomorrow night."

Yet, when the next night came, it was still cloudy. And so it was on the next night and the next.

One of the Hasidim said, "Maybe we should wait until next month to bless the moon."

Another said, "Maybe we should say the prayer even if we can't see the moon."

Finally, the Hasidim brought the problem to their Rebbe.

The Rebbe listened and took a few minutes to think.

The Rebbe said, "I have an idea, but first I need to make a phone call. I'll be back soon."

When the Rebbe returned, he said, "Let's each of us put $50 dollars on the table." There were a lot of Hasidim there, so it was quite a lot of money, but no one knew what the Rebbe was planning.

"Get into your cars and follow me," the Rebbe told them.

So the Hasidim got into their cars and drove for about an hour until the Rebbe, in the lead car, had his driver slow down. When the Rebbe saw the precise place to stop and park, the other cars also parked. It was very dark and no one else was in the parking lot.

The Rebbe told everyone, "Wait here." Then he left, without telling where he was going. Still, no one knew what the Rebbe was planning.

The Rebbe's idea was about to unfold. He took all the money that the Hasidim had put on the table, and went to the office of a helicopter company to pay for the special flight he booked on the phone.

After some time, the Rebbe came back, and led the Hasidim to a helipad, which was near the parking lot. It was so dark that no one had even noticed the helipad.

Soon they heard noise in the sky, but could not see anything. Then, they saw a helicopter getting ready to land.

The Rebbe told them, "This helicopter is for us! When the helicopter is on the ground, get in quickly." As the Hasidim were climbing aboard, the pilot reminded them to fasten their seat belts. The Rebbe sat next to the pilot, and whispered his plan to him.

When the rotor blades started to spin very fast, the pilot lifted off the helipad.

The Hasidim were looking at each other anxiously. Some of them had never flown in a helicopter.

The Rebbe's plan was actually a flight plan. Following his instructions, the pilot flew the helicopter until they were high above the thick, dark clouds.

When he spied their bright destination, the pilot turned the helicopter and hovered in one place so that everyone could clearly see the bright and glowing moon.

The Hasidim understood the amazing plan of their Rebbe, and everyone stood up.

Then the Rebbe said, "Now we can say *Kiddush Levana*, bless the moon!"

To bless the new moon at the proper time is like greeting the Divine Presence.
Talmud, Sanhedrin 42a

Aba continued, "Pops never knew why the Hasid chose to tell him that story, but he did know that his English teacher was like that Rebbe in the helicopter."

By always telling him that his work was "Very good," Mrs. Garb showed Pops the way to the moon – to his own light – even though there were so many dark clouds covering it. Just like the Rebbe showed the Hasidim their way – a way to the moon's light.

The Hasidim transformed the small aircraft into a Holy Helicopter. Holy because it lifted them up beyond the dark clouds to see the light.

Then Ima asked us, "Do you know anyone who acts like a Holy Flier?"

Aba said, "I know."

"Who?" Ima asked.

"You!" Aba answered. "I will explain. The other day I came home from work and I was so tired. It was a long day and my boss wasn't happy with the work I had done. I was feeling down.

"And then you said that I looked like I had a cloud over my head and you reminded me how good I am at my job. You believed in me and I felt so much better."

Ima smiled and asked again, "Who else knows a Holy Flier?"

I said, "I have a friend who sat with me during recess when I was upset. She reminded me about some of the good things I had done. I guess she is a Holy Flier because she encouraged me and her words helped me to feel much better."

"Yes," Ima said, "friends like that are surely Holy Fliers."

Shayna, what are the two words Aba said we have to memorize?
I CAN! ... I CAN!

It has been a long time since that windy evening on our back porch when Aba told us Pops' story.

I have met people who are Holy Fliers and I also try to be a Holy Flier – trying to lift people above the dark clouds in their lives and give them encouragement.

There is a saying that "Friends are like angels who lift us up when we have forgotten that our own wings know how to fly." Friends like that are Holy Fliers.

Today, I am an Ima. When it is time to say *Kiddush Levana,* I like to go out on our porch with my kids and look up to the sky. Sometimes I wonder if I might actually see a Holy Helicopter soaring there.

Questions for Conversation

- What can you learn from this story?

- What helps people act like Holy Fliers?

- What makes it difficult for people to act like Holy Fliers?

- Who has been a Holy Flier in your life?

- Which of your friends needs you to be a Holy Flier for them?

- How can you be a Holy Flier for that person?

Also By Josh (Yehoshua) Rubin

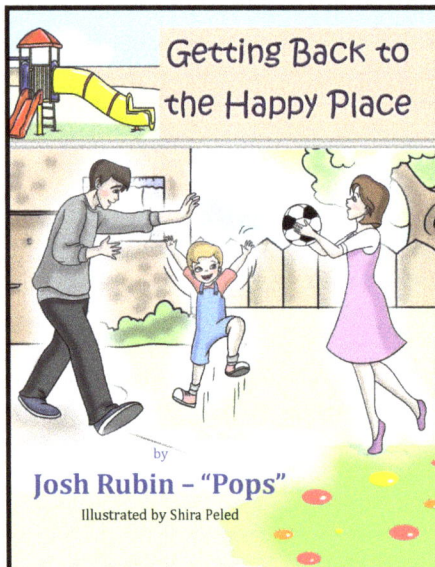

Getting Back to the Happy Place

by
Josh Rubin – "Pops"
Illustrated by Shira Peled

חזרה
למקום השמח בי

נכתב ע"י
יהושע רוביו
(המכונה "פופס" ע"י נכדיו)
איורים: שירה פלד

Getting Back To The Happy Place
English and Hebrew

www.ingramcontent.com/pod-product-compliance
Lightning Source LLC
LaVergne TN
LVHW070839080426
835512LV00025B/3485